smart investing
@ your library®

A partnership between American Library Association
and FINRA Investor Education Foundation

ALA American Library Association

FINra Investor Education FOUNDATION

FINRA is proud to support the American Library Association

BIG BUCK BU$INESS

SOCIAL NETWORKING
BIG BUSINESS ON YOUR COMPUTER

by Nick Hunter

Gareth Stevens
Publishing

Please visit our website, www.garethstevens.com. For a free color catalog of all our high-quality books, call toll free 1-800-542-2595 or fax 1-877-542-2596.

Library of Congress Cataloging-in-Publication Data

Hunter, Nick.
Social networking : big business on your computer / Nick Hunter.
    p. cm. — (Big-buck business)
Includes index.
ISBN 978-1-4339-7768-8 (pbk.)
ISBN 978-1-4339-7769-5 (6-pack)
ISBN 978-1-4339-7767-1 (library binding)
1. Online social networks—Economic aspects. 2. Social media—Economic aspects. 3. Internet advertising. 4. Business enterprises—Computer networks. I. Title.
HM742.H864 2013
006.7'54—dc23

2012002829

First Edition

Published in 2013 by
Gareth Stevens Publishing
111 East 14th Street, Suite 349
New York, NY 10003

Produced by Calcium Creative Ltd
Designed by Nick Leggett
Edited by Sarah Eason and Vicky Egan
Picture research by Susannah Jayes

Photo credits: Cover: Dreamstime: Hongqi Zhang cl; Shutterstock: Veronika Rumko cl, Valdis Torms cr, Takayuki cr. Inside: Paul Clark: 8cr; Devin Cook: 6bl; Dreamstime: Jacek Chabraszewski 29tr, Danieloizo 10b, Gruffydd Thomas 32b, Marcellofar 28br, Daniele Taurino 15t, Vlue 9b, Wrangler 3, 44b; Istockphoto: Sherwin McGehee 23r; Guillaume Paumier: 40cl; Spotify: 36br; Shutterstock: Yuri Arcurs 21br, A Turner 19cr, Carme Balcells 19tr, Bullet74 42bl, Cinemafestival 17tr, Conrado 31tr, Cristovao 19tcr, Djem 13tr, Elena Elisseeva 19tcmr, 38bl, Helga Esteb 24cl, Goodluz 37br, Richard Griffin 13br, Jorg Hackemann 19cmrr, Christopher Halloran 25tr, Holbox 19bmr, Blend Images 12r, Monkey Business Images 14b, Kenjito 33cl, Layland Masuda 19tmr, Miks 20–21c, Photobank.kiev.ua 30r, Pistolseven 4cl, Omer N Raja 45br, RoxyFer 16t, Annette Shaff 18b, Rui Vale de Sousa 19tcmrr, Jason Stitt 34br, Konstantin Sutyagin 19tmrr, SVLuma 4bl, Takayuki 22cr, Pit Tan 43t, Testing 39b, Liviu Toader 7br, Kiselev Andrey Valerevich 27br, Wavebreakmedia ltd 5l, 1000 Words 41t, Andy Z. 7l; Yahoo: 10t; You Tube: 25tr.

Printed in the United States of America

CPSIA compliance information: Batch #CS12GS: For further information contact Gareth Stevens, New York, New York at 1-800-542-2595.

CONTENTS

Introduction: Life Online   4
Chapter 1: Home Computers   6
Birth of the Internet   8
The First "Dotcom" Boom   10
Web 2.0   12
Chapter 2: What Is a Social Network?   14
Find Your Friends   16
Facebook Effect   18
Chapter 3: A World of Social Networks   20
The Blogosphere   22
Twitter and Other Microblogs   24
Sharing Videos and Music   26
Gaming   28
Chapter 4: Making Money from Social Networks 30
Online Advertising   32
The Value of Data   34
The Freemium   36
Chapter 5: The Big Players   38
Social Network Billionaires   40
Funding the Boom   42
Conclusion: Challenges Ahead   44
Glossary   46
For More Information   47
Index   48

LIFE ONLINE

The Internet has changed the way we live. We can use it to plan days out in our local area or a vacation on the other side of the world. We can shop online or sell things we don't need any more. The Internet has also changed the way we communicate with each other.

Online takes over

The change began when we started sending email messages rather than calling someone up or meeting face to face. People found it easier to communicate with instant messaging and online chatrooms. Since 2000, hundreds of millions of people have joined social networks.

Online, people can now meet, talk, and share photos, music, and every detail of their lives.

4

Big business industry

The social networking industry has grown very quickly to provide these services. Facebook was started in a college dorm in 2004, but by 2011, had nearly 1 billion users.

FUTURE FACT

In 2011, a survey found that Americans spent more than 53 billion minutes on Facebook, or about 3 hours a month for every man, woman, and child in the United States. Use of Facebook and other social networks is still growing.

In May 2010, people spent more than twice as much time on Facebook as on any other website.

CHAPTER 1

HOME COMPUTERS

The Internet has brought dramatic changes.
A 1980s office, school, or home would have had one or more personal computers (PCs), but they were basic and difficult to use compared to today's technology. They were mostly used by people with a special interest in computing or word processing.

The arrival of PCs

In the late 1970s, businesses such as Apple and software company Microsoft started to make personal computers (PCs) and programs that ordinary people could use. They weren't very powerful by today's standards, but people began buying them for use at home and at work.

During the 1980s, computer companies improved the look of PCs and made them more user-friendly.

Linking up

In 1990, most home and business computers could only share information with other computers if they were connected by a network cable. This all changed with the launch of the World Wide Web.

Many of the computing industry's pioneers were based in an area called Silicon Valley in California.

WORLD'S RICHEST PERSON

The people who launched the personal computer industry made a great deal of money. Bill Gates, founder and creator of Microsoft, became the world's richest person. Gates has used much of his wealth to fight poverty and disease around the world.

BIRTH OF THE INTERNET

The Internet was first developed in the 1980s. It allowed computer users in different government and research locations to link their computers to each other. In 1993, the US government first allowed businesses to use the Internet. The Internet Age had begun.

Information superhighway

Businesses soon realized that they could make money from the "information superhighway," as the World Wide Web was known in the 1990s. Internet service providers gave users access to the web and email. Other companies developed software that helped users browse the web.

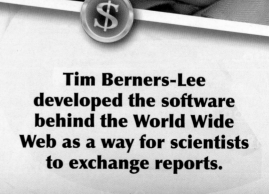

Tim Berners-Lee developed the software behind the World Wide Web as a way for scientists to exchange reports.

Making the web work for business

The first websites were mostly information providers. Yahoo! started as a list of recommended websites. It grew to include a search engine, information on topics such as business, and services including email. Yahoo! and AOL (America Online) tried to attract as many users as possible by offering free information and services.

Mail services have suffered because we send more communications by electronic mail than by conventional mail.

THE FIRST "DOTCOM" BOOM

By the late 1990s, millions of people were using the World Wide Web. New businesses were set up to make money from online customers. One of the biggest was Amazon.com, which started by selling books and then added other products. Internet traffic grew rapidly, people started using email, and every business had to have a website.

Amazon.com was started by Jeff Bezos in 1994. It has become one of the world's biggest retailers.

Online businesses multiply

Investors soon realized that online companies were worth putting money into. Online stores could reach customers all over the world, and other companies could reach the same people by advertising on the stores' websites.

Dotcoms

Investors rushed to put money into companies that added ".com" to their name. Most of the companies in the dotcom boom of the 1990s were online versions of traditional stores and businesses. The boom in the value of dotcom businesses reached its peak in spring 2000.

BUST!

At their peak, dotcom businesses were considered to be worth millions of dollars, even though their sales came to little more than a small store's. When investors realized that many would never make money, the value of dotcom stocks fell sharply, and many companies went bust.

WEB 2.0

From 2000 on, more and more people became Internet users. Faster Internet connections replaced slow dial-up connections. This meant that web users could download larger audio and video files from the web. Users could also upload their own photos and videos to share with friends.

Your words and pictures

A new type of online business, known as Web 2.0, developed. Web 2.0 businesses relied on customers to provide the words, pictures, and other features of their websites. Examples of Web 2.0 include social networking sites, blogs, wikis, and video-sharing sites.

The social web

Users soon discovered that through the web they could connect with old and new friends in a "social network." More and more people signed up to sites such as Myspace and Facebook. If their friends were on one of these sites, they had to be, too!

Affordable technology enables ordinary people to make and upload their own movies.

The music industry has changed greatly as people now listen to and share music online.

FUTURE FACT

Many retail businesses, such as travel agencies and bookstores, have moved their business online and closed their street stores. In the future, more industries, such as advertising, are likely to be affected by the success of social networks.

CHAPTER 2

WHAT IS A SOCIAL NETWORK?

A social network is a website that people use to connect to, and communicate with, friends. People mainly use social networks to share photos and talk online. In this chapter, we look at how social networking sites have changed our lives.

Previous generations socialized face-to-face. More and more people today are using social networking to make friends.

Why do people belong to social networks?

They join because they like to make connections or friendships. A social network allows us to keep in touch with people, no matter how little or how often we see them. It allows us to share our interests and find out more about our friends.

FUTURE FACT

We use social networks to write articles or upload our own music. Today, fewer budding journalists bother to try and get their work accepted by newspapers or magazines. Will the Internet completely replace paper versions of music and literature in the future?

Video chat means you can see the person you are talking to, wherever they are. Communication through social networks is usually free.

Networks need people

Customers are essential for any business, and this is also true of social networks. Without customers, social networks could not make money, so they try to attract as many people as possible.

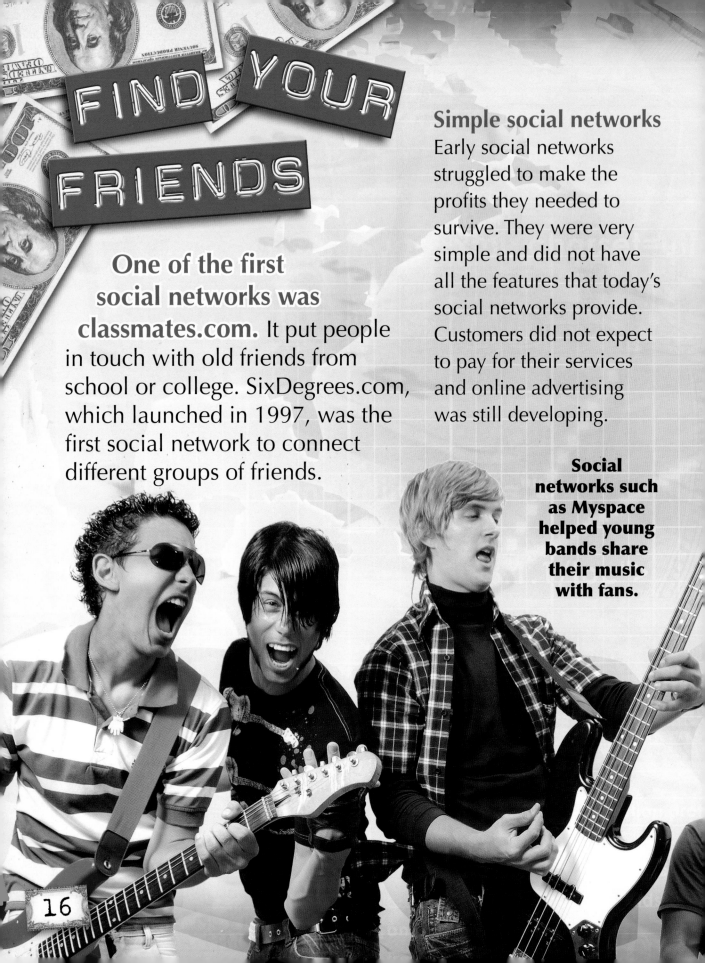

FIND YOUR FRIENDS

One of the first social networks was classmates.com. It put people in touch with old friends from school or college. SixDegrees.com, which launched in 1997, was the first social network to connect different groups of friends.

Simple social networks

Early social networks struggled to make the profits they needed to survive. They were very simple and did not have all the features that today's social networks provide. Customers did not expect to pay for their services and online advertising was still developing.

Social networks such as Myspace helped young bands share their music with fans.

Friendster

After 2000, things changed very quickly. Friendster, a social networking site, was launched. It became popular with users in technology and software industries. It was soon overtaken, however, by the network called Myspace.

Rupert Murdoch recognized the importance of social networking for the future of his vast media business.

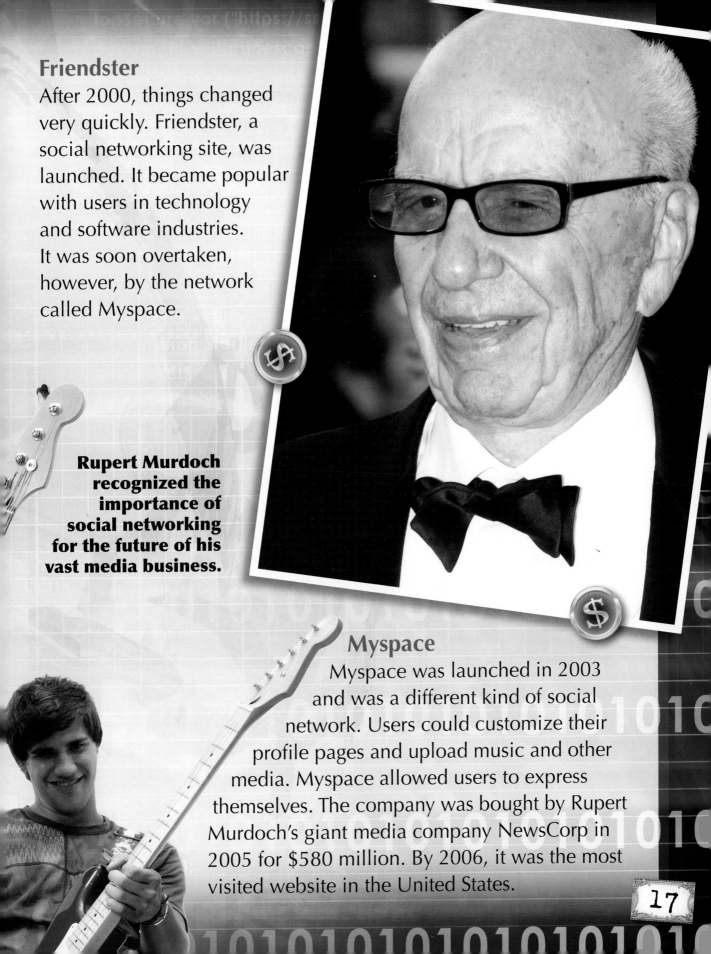

Myspace

Myspace was launched in 2003 and was a different kind of social network. Users could customize their profile pages and upload music and other media. Myspace allowed users to express themselves. The company was bought by Rupert Murdoch's giant media company NewsCorp in 2005 for $580 million. By 2006, it was the most visited website in the United States.

FACEBOOK EFFECT

A rival social network to Myspace appeared in 2004. Student Mark Zuckerberg started "the facebook" as a way for students at Harvard University to connect with each other. It grew rapidly and began to pick up new users by the millions. By the end of 2011, Facebook had more than 800 million users.

Facebook profiles

Setting up a profile on Facebook is very simple. Once set up, users can add applications and features to make their profile as complex as they want. This has made Facebook popular with everyone, from grandmothers to high school students.

Starting in 2006, anyone over the age of 13 with an email address could have their own Facebook profile.

Heading out? Stay connected
Visit facebook.com on your mobile ph

Facebook grows

As Facebook became more popular, Myspace declined. Facebook now wants to provide users with more ways to connect and share things online. It has linked to the music service Spotify so that users can see what their friends are listening to.

People from every generation and many different social backgrounds use Facebook.

FUTURE FACT

The more time people spend on Facebook, the more Facebook finds out about its users. It can use this information to sell advertising and make money in other ways.

CHAPTER 3

A WORLD OF SOCIAL NETWORKS

Facebook is the biggest social network, but it has many competitors. Lots of other online businesses want some of the success that Facebook has had.

For many people, online social networks are as important as the social network provided by their local community.

TAKE CARE WHAT YOU SHARE

Personal information is used by social media companies to make money. However, it may also be used by criminals. This means it is very important to be careful what personal information you share and whom you share it with.

Fighting Facebook

Some social networks deliberately do things differently from Facebook in order to attract users. Google+ was launched by the Internet giant Google, which controls the business of online searching and advertising. Users of Google+ can create separate groups, or "circles," of friends, such as school friends or family. They can then share different things with their different groups.

Filling a need

Some social networks try to satisfy particular groups of users. LinkedIn, for example, helps business people to make and share contacts, and has added features such as job postings. Other social networks are popular in particular regions. Orkut, owned by Google, is the most successful social network in India and Brazil.

Making connections with other businesspeople is important in many industries.

THE BLOGOSPHERE

Blogs are often linked to social network websites. Short for "web log," they range from respected pieces of writing on special subjects to a person's thoughts about what they did that day. If you subscribe to a blog, you are told by email when the next installment of the blog is available to read.

All kinds of blog

There are millions of blogs on the web on every subject, from music to politics. Many are personal, while others are written to support a business. Some blogs advertise related businesses that may be of interest to their readers.

Blogs enable people to share their interests or knowledge with people all over the world.

A question of trust

Blogs and social networks both provide an alternative to traditional media, such as newspapers and television. They are successful because people enjoy being updated with information and suggestions or tips from people they trust.

Reading the news in a printed newspaper may one day be a thing of the past.

FUTURE FACT

Between 2007 and 2009, sales of newspapers in the United States fell by 30 percent. In order to keep their readers, many newspapers now offer their information online as well as in print, and more are likely to do so in the future.

TWITTER AND OTHER MICROBLOGS

A microblog is similar to a blog, but has much less information. The best-known microblogging service is Twitter, which was started in 2006 by Evan Williams and Biz Stone. Twitter users can send short messages, called tweets, to their followers, and follow tweets posted by other users. Many celebrities and businesses use microblogs.

A good business?

Being able to reach a community of customers is valuable for many businesses. Twitter has more than 300 million users, but some people question whether microblogging businesses will be able to make money from their users.

Celebrities such as Justin Bieber can talk directly to their millions of followers on Twitter.

On location

Smartphones have made the Internet mobile. People use them to connect to the Internet when they are out and about. This has led to the creation of a location-based social networking website called foursquare.com. Users can log their favorite locations, and local advertisers can sell products to them.

USEFUL FOR BUSINESS

Social networks are important tools for businesses. By attracting friends and followers on social networks, businesses can create communities of customers, whom they can target with advertising and offers. They may also get useful feedback and ideas from their customers.

Barack Obama was one of the first politicians to realize the importance of social networks in his presidential campaign.

SHARING VIDEOS AND MUSIC

Sharing music and videos is an important part of social networks. If sites such as Facebook can persuade people to watch videos on their website, customers will spend more time on the site.

In 2006, YouTube was bought by Google for $1.6 billion.

Video king

YouTube is the biggest video platform on the web. Users upload their personal videos to YouTube, and viewers watch the videos online or share them via a social network. Like many social networking sites, users can visit YouTube without paying a cent.

Super growth

YouTube was started in 2005. By the summer of 2006, it was already hosting 25 million videos. By 2010, the company could boast that 24 hours of new video were uploaded every minute!

Myspace and music

Like video, music plays a big part in social networking. Myspace has specialized in being a great way for new artists to get their music to a wider audience.

FUTURE FACT

People can now stream music and videos. They no longer need to download the files, which saves them money. According to one survey, people who listen to streamed music are less likely to share music files illegally.

GAMING

The computer revolution brought with it computer games. The first online games appeared in the late 1990s. As broadband Internet connections got faster, the gaming industry boomed. By 2010, Microsoft's Xbox Live network had 20 million users.

Multiplayer online games

One of the most popular online games is World of Warcraft. Players compete against each other or work together in groups to complete tasks. They can "chat," or talk, online to other players, making the game a social experience.

In 2011, World of Warcraft had more than 11 million players.

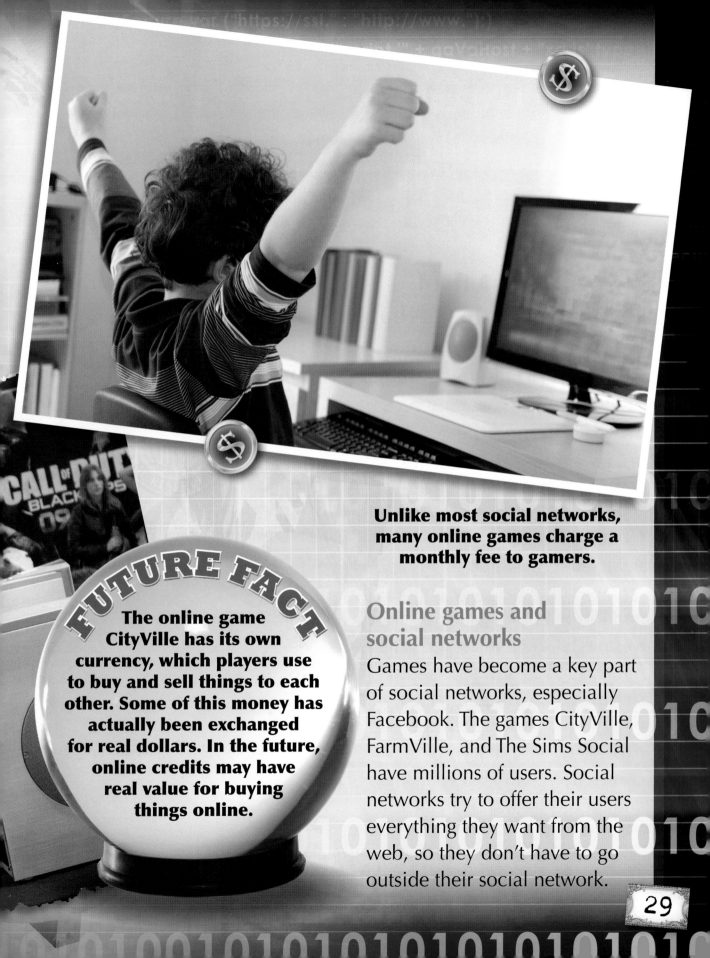

Unlike most social networks, many online games charge a monthly fee to gamers.

Online games and social networks

Games have become a key part of social networks, especially Facebook. The games CityVille, FarmVille, and The Sims Social have millions of users. Social networks try to offer their users everything they want from the web, so they don't have to go outside their social network.

MAKING MONEY FROM SOCIAL NETWORKS

A great feature of social networking is that it's free. You can create a Facebook profile or start using Twitter without paying a cent. This has helped the biggest social networks to attract huge numbers of users.

Costing money

A social network has to pay for offices, computer programmers, and lots of computers and servers to store all the photos and other information that users want to share. So how does it make enough money to pay these expenses? Most of its money comes from selling advertising and credits for online games.

Social network entrepreneurs can make millions from investors if their networks can attract enough users.

Users are happy to sign up to a social network that keeps them in touch with friends, so long as they don't have to pay.

Keeping it free

The most successful social networks know that the more users they have, the more opportunities they have to sell advertising. If the networks started charging for their services, their users would probably sign up with a free rival network instead.

ONLINE ADVERTISING

Social networks use advertising to make money. Internet advertising can be aimed much more closely than commercials on television, which may not be seen by the right people.

Social networks can provide advertisers with valuable, detailed information about possible customers.

Targeting the market

Advertisers try to target their advertisements at people who are most likely to buy their products. Google has been very successful at linking advertising with the searches people make for specific words on their search engine.

How much do you reveal?

Do you have a social network profile? Think about all the things that the company providing the service knows about you from your profile. It knows your age, where you live, and what businesses or celebrities you follow. The more information you share online, the more useful you are to the social network because it can target you with advertising that fits your profile.

Every time you click on an advertisement, it tells social networking businesses a little more about you.

FUTURE FACT

In 2011, about $30 billion, or 15 cents in every advertsing dollar, was spent on online advertising in the United States. By 2015, it is estimated that this figure will have risen to 30 cents in every dollar.

THE VALUE OF DATA

What is the main product that a social network has to sell? It's not the service itself, because that's free. The main product is you! The network provider collects all the data about you that it can and passes on the information to advertisers.

Businesses, recruiters, and colleges can find out about you from social networks. Take care what you share!

Who benefits?

Advertisers use the data they get from social networks to target products at people. Businesses also use it to design new products that they think people will want to buy in the future.

Personal recommendations on social networks are a great way for businesses to attract new customers.

The personal touch

If you're looking for a good place to eat out, you might do an online search, but you're just as likely to ask a friend if they can recommend somewhere. A business such as a restaurant will advertise "special offers" online to attract customers. It hopes the customers will then recommend it to their friends.

PRIVACY

Many people are happy to give up some of their privacy for the benefits that a social network brings. Other people believe that customers should be given more information about how their personal data is being used.

THE FREEMIUM

Social networks can make money by charging customers for special services. Networks that do this are called "freemium" businesses. The idea is that most customers can use the service for free, but a small number of users who use the service a lot or who want to use special features have to pay. The paying customers cover the costs of the service and ensure it makes money.

More for your money

Social networks that offer freemium services know that only a small number of their many users are likely to pay for the special premium services. The business network LinkedIn offers paying customers greater access to the millions of businesspeople who use the network. It's a valuable service to people who want to make new contacts.

Spotify

Buying credits

Facebook makes money by selling credits that are used in online games. Only a small number of its users pay for these, but Facebook has so many users that this adds up to hundreds of millions of dollars.

Spotify's users can listen to some music without paying or pay a monthly fee to listen as much as they want.

Paying for premium access to social networks helps salespeople find more customers and make more money.

CHAPTER 5

THE BIG PLAYERS

Social networking is still a very young industry. The world's biggest social networks have only been running since 2000. Many of them have not yet made a profit, as the costs of attracting and providing a service to millions of users are so high.

Big money

Out of Apple, Microsoft, and Google, only Google has invested lots of money in social networks and media, including Google+, YouTube, and Brazil's Orkut network. Google has proved that it can make big money from online advertising. This is not yet the case with many of its rivals.

Companies that advertise on social networking sites can attract huge sales of their products.

Facebook adds features

Although Google makes big money from its social network, it offers fewer services than the biggest social networks. Facebook dominates the industry and continues to add new features to hold the interest of its users. Twitter also became popular by offering a different kind of social network.

Google has tried to compete with Facebook by linking social networking to its other services, such as its search engine.

Google 谷歌

SOCIAL NETWORK BILLIONAIRES

The biggest players in social networking are said to be worth hundreds of millions or even billions of dollars. How did they get to be so rich, when many of the social networking businesses they run do not yet make a profit?

The face of Facebook

The most famous figure in the world of social networking is Mark Zuckerberg, the founder of Facebook. In 2011, Zuckerberg was said to be worth $13.5 billion at the age of just 27. This is based on the value of Facebook as a business if Zuckerberg decided to sell it. In 2010, *Time* magazine named Zuckerberg as its Person of the Year, pointing out that if all Facebook's users were in one country, it would be the third biggest country in the world!

Mark Zuckerberg of Facebook has been learning Chinese so that he doesn't miss out on a billion possible customers.

Google+

Search Google+

+You

Social networking is just part of Google's giant technology business.

Search engine stars

Larry Page and Sergey Brin founded Google, the most popular search engine on the web. Google makes billions of dollars from online advertising. The Google+ social network is likely the biggest threat to Facebook.

Biggest bloggers

Biz Stone and Evan Williams founded the blogging service Blogger.com in 1999. Not content with that, they went on to found Twitter with Jack Dorsey. Twitter is said to be worth billions of dollars.

FUNDING THE BOOM

The biggest players in social networking were all still in their twenties when they had ideas that would change the world. To make their ideas reality, they needed money.

Taking a risk

Venture capitalists are people who put money into new businesses. They'll give money to a new business in exchange for owning part of the company. It's a risky thing to do because many new companies do not survive and very few achieve the sort of success that Facebook has had.

Venture capitalists can provide the money that social networks need to become global players.

Investors in social networks are keen to see their networks expand into new regions, such as China and India.

Making a profit

Investors in a new business hope that the business will be successful so they can share the profits. A successful business may buy up other companies. Google, for example, paid $1.6 billion to buy YouTube in 2006. A business can also raise money by selling shares of the business to the public.

CHALLENGES AHEAD

In less than a decade, social networks have become a huge part of our lives. We already use Facebook and other networks for communication, leisure, and gaming, and the big players in the industry would like us to use their networks even more.

Making money

The biggest challenge for social networks is turning their millions of users into profits through advertising. Will people be happy if their profile pages are cluttered with ads or if they have to pay for features that were once free? Social networks think they will be.

Almost half of all users now visit social networks through their phones.

Love it or hate it...

Millions of people are happy to give up some privacy in return for the benefits of social networking. Many people, however, worry that there is not enough privacy protection. Although an unhappy customer can easily switch to another social network, they cannot easily take their network of friends with them. One thing is for sure—however much privacy is an issue, social networking is here to stay.

Social networking is changing fast. Somewhere, an entrepreneur is developing a new social network, hoping to capture millions of users.

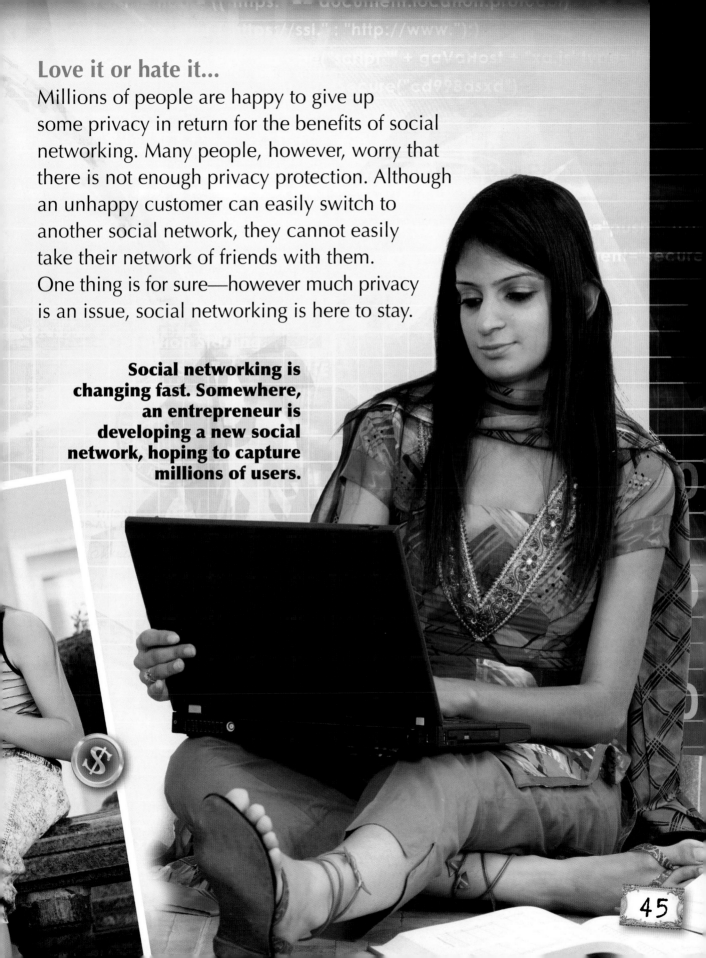

GLOSSARY

AOL (America Online) technology company that provides Internet services

Apple technology company that, since 2000, has created computers, music players, phones, and other products

blogs short for web logs

broadband high-speed Internet connection that enables users to access video and other services online

browse process of viewing or clicking between different websites

chatroom online service that lets users communicate with instant messages

credit token or electronic voucher that can be used online instead of money

currency form of money, such as US dollars or Japanese yen

customize change to suit the needs of a particular user

dial-up connection slow Internet connection made by dialing a phone number

email message that is sent electronically via the Internet

hosting providing a "place" on the Internet for a website

Internet connection link between a computer and the Internet. It connects a computer to millions of other computers.

Internet service provider (ISP) company that provides computer users with an Internet connection

Internet traffic the flow of data across the Internet

messaging creating and exchanging short messages, such as emails, using a computer. Instant messaging is like a telephone conversation that uses text-based, not voice-based, communication.

network cable cable that connects a computer to a network of other computers. Computers connected by a wireless connection do not need a network cable.

platform operating system on which a program or device runs

posted put on the Internet

profile user's personal page on a social network and the information it contains

profits money that a business makes on top of the money it has spent or invested

search engine a computer program that searches web pages for a specific word and supplies a list of the documents where that word was found

shares parts of a company that can be bought or sold on a stock market

smartphone cell phone that can connect to the Internet and run other applications

stocks shares in the value of a business or company. People who buy stock own a part of a business.

stream send video or audio files in a continuous stream of data, which the user plays as it arrives, live over the Internet

upload transfer a file from a personal computer to the Internet so it can be viewed by others

wiki website or document that many users can add data to or edit

FOR MORE INFORMATION

BOOKS

Hile, Lori. *Social Networks and Blogs* (Mastering Media series). Chicago, IL: Heinemann-Raintree, 2011.

Hillstrom, Laurie Collier. *Online Social Networks*. Farmington Hills, MI: Lucent Books, 2010.

Lusted, Marcia Anidon. *Mark Zuckerberg: Facebook Creator* (Essential Lives series). Edina, MN: ABDO Publishing, 2011.

Sutherland, Adam. *Facebook* (Big Business series). London, UK: Wayland, 2011.

WEBSITES

Find out more about social networking at:

www.netlingo.com

www.facebook.com/zuck

You can also discover more about social networking on social networking websites themselves, such as Twitter or Google+. Look for section with headings such as "about this site" or "company info."

Publisher's note to educators and parents: Our editors have carefully reviewed these websites to ensure that they are suitable for students. Many websites change frequently, however, and we cannot guarantee that a site's future contents will continue to meet our high standards of quality and educational value. Be advised that students should be closely supervised whenever they access the Internet.

INDEX

advertising 11, 13, 16, 19, 20, 22, 25, 30, 31, 32, 33, 34, 38, 41, 44
Amazon.com 10
America Online 9
Apple 6, 31, 38

Berners-Lee, Tim 8
Bezos, Jeff 10
blog/blogs 12, 22, 23, 24
Blogger.com 41
Brazil 21, 38
Brin, Sergey 41
broadband 28

chatrooms 4
classmates.com 16

Dorsey, Jack 41

email 4, 8, 9, 10, 18, 22

Facebook 5, 13, 18, 19, 20, 26, 29, 30, 31, 37, 39, 40, 41, 42, 43, 44
foursquare.com 25
freemium services 36
Friendster 17

games 28–29, 30, 37, 44
Gates, Bill 7
Google 20, 21, 26, 31, 33, 38, 39, 41, 43
Google+ 20, 38, 41

India 21, 43
instant messaging 4

LinkedIn 21, 36

microblogs 24
Microsoft 6, 7, 28, 38
Murdoch, Rupert 17
Myspace 13, 16, 17, 18, 19, 27, 37

NewsCorp 17
newspapers 15, 23

Orkut 21, 38

Page, Larry 41
privacy 35, 45
profile pages 17, 44
profits 16, 38, 40, 43, 44

search engines 9, 33, 39, 41
SixDegrees.com 16
smartphones 25, 44
Spotify 19, 37
streaming music and video 27
Stone, Biz 24, 41

Twitter 24, 30, 39, 41

United States 5, 17, 23, 33, 39

venture capitalists 42, 43
video sharing 12, 26

Web 2.0 12
Williams, Evan 24, 41
World of Warcraft 28

Xbox Live 28

Yahoo! 9, 11
YouTube 26, 27, 38, 43

Zuckerberg, Mark 18, 40